£3

Revealed

Carolyn Quartermaine

Revealed

photography by JACQUES DIRAND

text by KATE CONSTABLE

conran
OCTOPUS

First published in 2001 by Conran Octopus Limited
a part of Conran Publishing Group
2–4 Heron Quays
London E14 4JP
www.conran-octopus.co.uk

Text copyright © 1997 Carolyn Quartermaine
Special photography copyright © 1997 Jacques Dirand
and Carolyn Quartermaine
Design and layout copright © 2001 Conran Octopus

Commissioning Editor Bridget Hopkinson
Editor Christine Davies
Creative Director Leslie Harrington
Design Broadbase
Production Manjit Sihra

A catalogue record for this book is available from
the British Library

ISBN 1 84091 184 0

Printed and bound in Spain by Bookprint, S.L., Barcelona

contents

introduction by Donna Karan

Paths can cross in very strange ways, stirring energy in both a real-life way and in an artistic way, reaching from both sides of the Atlantic and across the continents.

Like every designer, I pull pages from magazines for inspiration and colour from other walks of life besides fashion, and we each in our own way find something stimulating and directional in these images. Returning to New York from London a while ago, I took with me some beautiful pages that spoke to me so much that I carried one picture around with me for over a year.

Back in London many months later, I was taken to meet an artist whom a friend said I must see. As I walked into the room I realized I had walked into the picture I had been carrying around. My first words were, 'Where is your gold cement bathtub?' The artist stared at me in utter amazement. I never saw the bathtub, but I found an artist who understood color, fabric and quality with a true sensitivity. It was my first meeting with Carolyn Quartermaine.

From the first moment, a relationship began — it was a great experience to see art and fashion coming together in fabrics, articulating the body in color, form and shape. We recognized our similar sensibilities — with an emphasis on art, inspired by antiquities, an understanding of the detailing and the patina — and I recognized Carolyn's individual touch and nuance.

Now I don't have to look through magazines for Carolyn's work — those tear sheets are highlighted and collected, inspiring at all times, in one place in this wonderful book. Enjoy!

the Total Look

*C*arolyn Quartermaine's look is one of pure romance. And although she seems to have plundered the past for inspiration, with lines of old-fashioned italic script dancing across the seat of a French Empire-style chair, her work is very much about the present. What characterizes her style is her ability to see beauty in the most unlikely objects and then to mix them with elegant eclecticism in the most delightful way. When Quartermaine decorates a room, it is as though one of her collages has come to life: disparate pieces are pulled together by an inspired use of colour, shape and texture. But behind this eclecticism lies a rigorous process of editing: Quartermaine likes to pare everything down to what she calls 'the best details'. And what might those details be? 'Pin a piece of paper on a wall and place a bergère chair in front, hang lovely fabric at the windows, add a good floor and some flowers… maybe that is all you need in any room for it to be beautiful,' she says.

My Angels Happy
Christmas, lots Love
from Paul X

"L'idée-image surréaliste
dans toute sa fraîcheur ori-
ginelle, pour moi, continue à
se découvrir en Maurice...
...y chaque fois qu'un mo-
...encore mal éveillée m'appo...
...la primeur d'un de ses dess...
dans le journal (et je suis ...
lors content, et je pense qu'il ...
...la belle manière—la sienne...
...nous avons compris le monde...
...un grand raison de soleil...
...primait je n'oublie dans les...
...eaux"
André Breton 1946

She saw an anim... ...ty, and ...guis
...ver winding near it along the plain, and ...
...stream went slowly gliding a boat with
...rry party of children on board—

which was lying a card
EAT   ME beautiful
...ng letter

un film de Jean Cocteau

Carolyn Quartermaine

Lettres personnelles

ANGLETERRE

Pour voi
n'en oublié
...FN pour
Reines de

'I adore France and I've always
been inspired by those classical
eighteenth-century and early
nineteenth-century French
interiors. The rooms are so restful,
very composed, very formal.'
Quartermaine is also drawn to the
purity of Scandinavian interiors.
'I like the way that Swedish rooms
look as if the colour has been
bleached out of them. They
borrowed a lot from the French –
the shapes and styles – but in using
plainer materials, the look became
less ornate.' Combining elements
from both traditions can create a
truly individual yet harmonious
environment (*left*).

You can't escape the fairy-tale
quality of the fabrics, furniture and
interiors that Quartermaine creates.
And while everything she touches
is not quite turned to gold, it is
dipped, dyed, embroidered and
gilded until it has gloss and lustre.
'I have a love of gold and pale grey.
It is a colour combination that
makes me think of French châteaux.
And drawing on that association,
I began to use gold in collages and
on fabrics. Its attraction is not just
the colour – there is the reflective
quality to it as well.' The result is not
just fairy-tale but also pure glamour.

'My home is my studio (*above*), and my rooms reveal my ideas in process… Life isn't at a standstill.' Quartermaine is drawn to artists' studios: 'We always view work in galleries; that is, clean spaces. It would be so wonderful to see the creative process as well as understanding the finished piece of work.' In her own studio, the whole space is transformed into an ever-changing collage of ideas, textures and colours (*left*).

Colour

Watching the way that Carolyn Quartermaine works with colour is to see much of the essence of her artistic vision exposed. 'When looking at anything, the first point of reference for me will be its colour,' she says. Everything that fascinates her, interests her or sets her off on a flight of the imagination can be traced back to her enjoyment of colour and to her highly individual colour syntax. Colour charts and theorizing play no part here, however: hers is a highly personal and emotional response. 'I think that everyone has a colour sense that is all their own,' she says. 'Of course, my knowledge has been expanded through training and art school, but my eye for colour, my palette, my taste... I feel I was born with it.' For Quartermaine, colours are as descriptive as words. She loves playing with vibrant hues, mixing tangerine with lilac, emerald green with copper, citrus yellow with hot pink in a brazen display of colourful chic. At the same time she is drawn to the ethereal and romantic quality of pale tones.

Quartermaine is highly sensitive to the effect colours have on each other and how colour combinations can create different moods. Orange, for instance, 'is such a joyous colour and has a way of enriching other things'. There is a shade of burnt orange that she associates particularly with Italy. 'Maybe it is because of the way orange absorbs light, but you can't help but look at it and feel heat,' she says. It also reminds her of Italian towns with their painted stucco walls, which she evokes by juxtaposing orange with more neutral hues.

'This is my version of a Klimt flower garden,' says Quartermaine of her dazzling wall display of silk drawstring bags. 'In looking at those paintings, the dots and dashes that make up the flower heads look like drops of pure colour.' By setting intense, distinct colours against a plain background she gives colour freedom to roam, allowing relationships to form between the strongly contrasting shades.

Colour is all about balance – knowing what to do with very strong colour, how to contain it and just when to stop. Quartermaine's gold 'French Script' design on this sofa, over-printed on a rich red and bordeaux stripe, gives depth to the colours, while the stripes provide structure. Offset by gold, red takes on historical resonances, reminiscent of imperial grandeur.

Although Quartermaine loves 'colour with spirit and verve', she rarely puts intense colour onto walls, preferring to leave them pale and to use deep colours on chairs and banners. Luxurious shades of grape, aubergine and cassis, enriched with swirls of gilt script, look elegant and refined when set against the dull grey of beautiful panelling. The mood is one of restrained splendour, as if an artist had chosen to suggest an idea through a line drawing rather than a fully painted canvas.

'I like colours that are alive, that are layered, that seem to contain themselves, and more.' By playing with the elements of a particular palette Quartermaine creates her own artistic update on a decorative style. She adds depth and texture to Swedish-style blue-grey paintwork by adding a wash of turquoise and a piece of rusted silk; the result is luscious without being heavy or overdone (*left*). She also speaks of what she calls 'fragile colour', 'the colour you get when you hang a length of silk organza at a window: you look through the fabric and the world takes on a slightly different hue' (*right*).

Paloma Beach

If Quartermaine were forced to choose any single colour over another, it would probably be a certain shade of blue-pink lilac. 'Lilac is elegant, serene, calming, spiritual and cleansing.' It is a shade that looks good not only when it is at its most translucent – as in a piece of tissue paper – but also in more intense incarnations, such as in a dye-saturated length of silk. The freshest colours are those found in flower petals; the stamens of the passion flower (*right*) look almost as if they have been dipped in pigment.

Shape

When Carolyn Quartermaine turns her attention to the subject of shape, there are very few compromises – and even fewer straight lines. For Quartermaine, 'shape demands the highest purity. No uncertainty, no fudging.' Looking at the things with which she has chosen to surround herself, you realize that the same shapes are repeated everywhere, similar forms are echoed, and fine lines appear in duplicate and triplicate, gorgeously gilded. 'Everything comes down to shape,' she says. 'For me, the way the light hits the crystal drops on a chandelier is unimportant if the shape of the chandelier is wrong in the first place.' Shape is also the key to the confident way she places together so many disparate objects, from different eras and different countries, to create a look that is completely her own. Eschewing surface 'style', her highly tuned eye sees through the surface of things to the structure beneath. Design pedants may baulk, but Quartermaine dances to an altogether more lyrical tune.

In Quartermaine's philosophy, 'shape is the soul of something, it animates things that have no life". She looks for shape that 'dances with movement and irresistibly draws the eye to it', such as the sensuous frame of a classic French chair (*above*). Her elegant lampshades have a flirty sweep, like the hem of a dress whooshed up and out by the swirl of a dancer's body (*right*).

Ne'mours

Madame.

Puis qu'entre tous.

les Princes Chrétiens —
auxquels la Principau-
-té de Neufchatel X
Valange a étés heureu —

Seigneur
frère

fois et beaucoup audessous
le nom et les plus puissans

...mona comma...
...couvremingnai...
...formea qu'on...
...osces sur tous les...

There is a lightness of touch to everything Quartermaine does, as if her creations could defy gravity. She likes shapes that look so fluid they could be sipped through a straw: 'I do not like anything that is hard-edged. I want to keep everything fluid and full of movement.' And so there are hand-drawn scrolls, swirls of embroidery, and fabric marked with fine italic script that looks as if it has been applied with a quill dipped in gold ink.

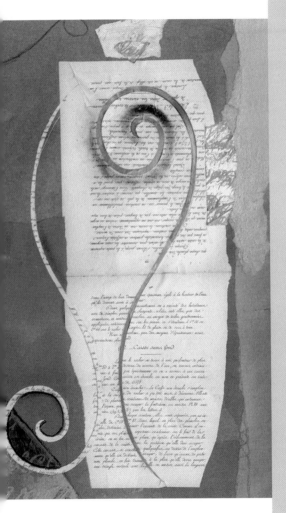

'Shape defines your taste because
of what it forces you to exclude. If
you are drawn to flowing lines, to
scrolls, to certain types of chair, for
example, immediately there is much
that will not interest you. And in
that process of the eye recognizing
what it likes, your taste is defined.'
Quartermaine's own taste has
been with her since childhood.
'I have always been attracted to the
same things – I think I have an
appreciation of fine, delicate,
I suppose some people would call
them feminine shapes. The whole
process for me is quite intuitive.'

'When I first went to art school, I started in the sculpture department. I loved making shapes, working with solid form. It was only because I could not do without colour that I moved across to painting.' While Quartermaine no longer sculpts, this training disciplined her eye to the point that, for her, a carved Louis XVI chair has all the qualities of a piece of sculpture (*left*). But there is nothing rigid about her sense of form: 'I adore shapes that are suggestive of other things. I don't like things that are too perfect, too finished." Hence her lovely reworking of Man Ray's famous photograph (*right*).

Fabric

*Q*uartermaine is an artist who uses fabrics to cross boundaries – between fashion and interiors, history and the present day. Historical allusions trail behind her like the train of a mannequin's gown, but these allusions are stitched according to a very modern taste. And like Elsa Schiaparelli, who cocooned herself in crêpe de Chine when she had no money for a ball dress, Quartermaine is able to whip, pin, catch and tie fabrics into a tantalizing array of fashionable chic. When designing her own textiles she is very much hands-on, going through the whole printing process herself before the designs are made up in larger quantities. 'I might start off with one idea,' she says, 'but when I physically start to print or paint the fabrics, something can take me off in another direction.' But Quartermaine is not really interested in base fabrics, straight off the roll. Like a disc jockey who samples and edits, she likes to cut, dye, slice and sew these fabrics until her world is covered in a luminous mosaic of shimmering cloth.

'Silk is my favourite fabric. It can be really vibrant… the colours are so true. And there is such luxury in the *shine*.' When Quartermaine set about creating a stage set of couture glamour in the stairwell of a fairy-tale French château, she knew that fabric would be the most important element in creating the effect she wanted. The results were intoxicating: a train of emerald silk falling down the stairs, curvaceous wicker mannequins wrapped in swathes of shocking pink and green. 'Almost any material can look good if used in a spirit of generosity,' says Quartermaine.

Spools of silk thread, ribbons, antique buttons – all of these are as beguiling to Quartermaine as a box of chocolates. Along with other tools of the couturier's trade, these artefacts provide an endless source of inspiration (*above*). And when her sewing box is empty, she simply unpacks her jewellery, which she has collected since she was a little girl (*right*).

'A piece of fabric can change everything… how you look and how you are.' The same goes for interiors, where Quartermaine sees fabrics not merely as a backdrop but as decorative surfaces in their own right. Costumes are taken out of the closet to be hung like paintings in a gallery, creating their own magic (*left*). An exquisite eighteenth-century gilet, with its delicate periwinkle-blue embroidery and lilac buttons, is pushed into another dimension when it is hung at a window and framed by sunshine. Even the stains and spots of age and wear possess their own beauty (*right*).

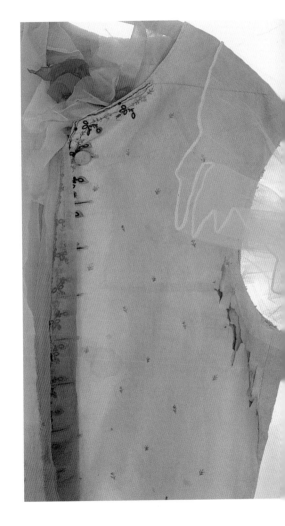

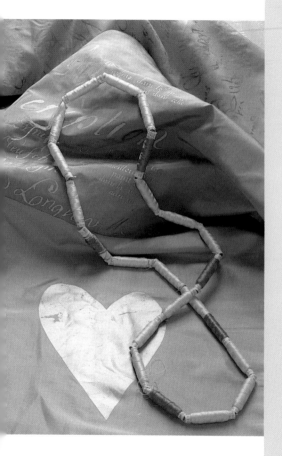

'Designing fabrics isn't an abstract thing. I achieve results by working through a process, but there is no formula to what I do.' Patterning with script, for example, happened in the early days when Quartermaine was designing paper for collages; she later translated the writing to silk. 'I put the fabric on a chair, and that's when it all took off.' The result was 'French Script', one of the most desirable and instantly recognizable fabric designs of the 1980s. An inventive use of fabric as a decorative surface has remained a Quartermaine hallmark ever since.

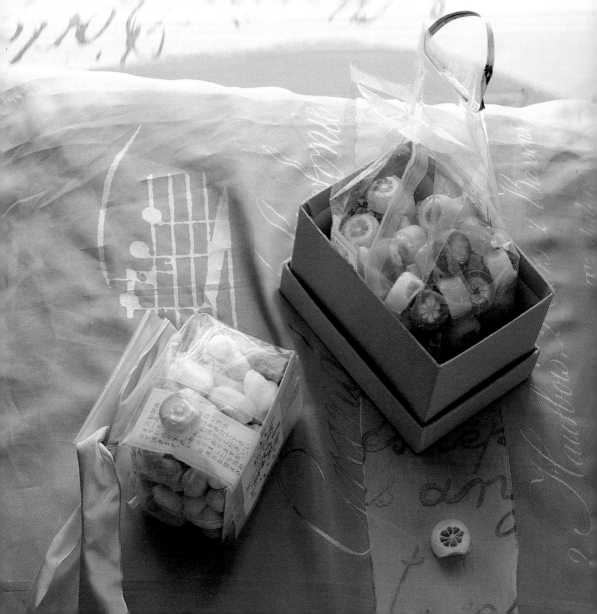

Paper

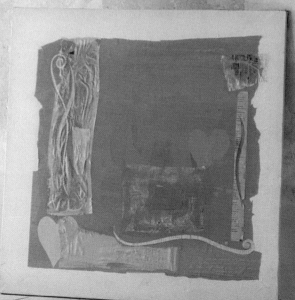

When it comes to paper, Quartermaine's tastes are catholic. She can be attracted to almost anything – from wispy sheets of tissue paper, which she gilds and scratches to make a surface that looks like an old looking glass, to fine brown wrapping paper, which is scored into rolls or used in large overlapping squares like a canvas for one of her collages. 'I have an obsession with paper,' she acknowledges. 'To me a piece of paper is as precious as a piece of silk.' This 'obsession' can be fuelled by any part of her life: the crinkly paper from an amaretto biscuit, an envelope bearing spidery handwriting, pages ripped from a French chemistry book... all are hoarded like treasure. And if materials are not beautiful to begin with she works hard until they are, stamping, printing and painting them until they take on a new surface pattern. The results are not only used to make two-dimensional collages: these delicate layers are applied to walls, doors and objects, giving a sense of the ethereal and the exotic.

Quartermaine's love of paper is not just about creating art, nor is it about an ability to create luxurious objects out of simple everyday things... this passion is more intrinsically a part of everyday life. 'I can spend hours cutting paper into tassels to ensure that something is beautifully wrapped. It becomes part of the present, part of the experience. The only problem is that having taken the trouble to wrap flowers in beautiful paper, and maybe tie them with a ribbon, you then see that paper discarded. To me the paper is just as beautiful as anything else.'

'I first found the blocks of "Toile Royale" writing paper in a department store in Paris when I was a student. At the time I couldn't really afford it: buying blocks of this exquisite paper just because of that embossed and gilded top sheet was sheer extravagance. But I knew instantly that I had to have it and would need it in a piece of work one day.' Once she has found her papers Quartermaine cuts, glues, waxes, gilds, tears and scratches them to create something that is not tied to any one place or time.

Quartermaine is a collage supremo,
producing pieces that look at once
antique and entirely modern.
And because of the diversity of
the papers that she uses, and the
techniques employed to make them
her own, these two-dimensional,
abstract works have great depth
and narrative quality. 'I find it
very difficult to think about paper
without thinking about collage.
With collage the end result is much
more than the sum of the parts.'

LETTRES
IMPÉRIALES

Even the most inexpensive papers are precious to Quartermaine. 'Brown paper, especially when it is surrounded by gilt, can look so luxurious'; when glued to silk, as part of a collage, it can also help 'fix' disparate elements. Her enthusiasm for collage has led to further experimentation with applying layers of paper to surfaces and to objects, which she glamorizes with exquisite gilding and delicious lines of text.

Paint

*C*arolyn Quartermaine is fascinated by paint; by the way it looks (when graffiti is scratched into a painted wall), by the way it behaves (sinking into paper, bleeding into other colours), and by what artists choose to do with it. She cites Mark Rothko and Craigie Aitchison among her many inspirations: 'What I love is the way those artists retain the quality of the paint they are using. It gives me a sense of freedom to look into a canvas so saturated with colour, so intense that it seems to pulsate.' As one might expect by looking at her work, Quartermaine's own approach is far from purist. She might mix up huge jars of pigments and dyes to paint panels for a collage; she might drop watered-down textile paint onto silk to represent flowers; or she might spend hours building up layers of watery emulsion to exaggerate existing defects on a wall. The thrill for her comes in trying to control the uncontrollable, 'in knowing when to pull back and when to let the paint do what it wants to do'.

Quartermaine's absorption in the process of painting is shown by an attachment to her tools and raw materials. 'Over the years, the jars in which I mix the paints have developed into something special in their own right. The tools of your trade become beautiful objects… I sometimes think that looking at an artist's palette can be as appealing as looking at the finished canvas.'

'For me, a good wall has the same
spellbinding quality as a Twombly
or a Rothko painting. I love the
mottled marks, the mould, the
flaking caused by pollution, the
scratch marks of the graffiti.' What
excites Quartermaine about these
walls is the same thing that she is
trying to create in her own collages.
'I am drawn to the feeling of time
passing, the feeling that paint has
been built up over the years and
then has been worn away again, by
chance, by weather, or by intent.'

'I have this immediate response when I see a bag of pigment or a jar of liquid colour. It is so powerful that even walking into a studio can set me thinking.' If Quartermaine is excited by the physical presence of paint, she is even more fascinated by how it behaves. 'The way the colours seep into each other, bleed into each other, is stunning. And you are always there watching, all the time, trying to control the wash of colour.'

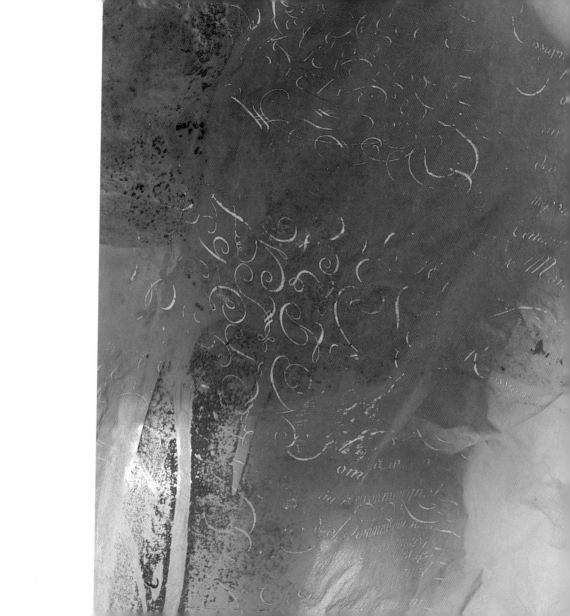

Flowers

*I*n the way she decorates with flowers, as with everything else she does, Quartermaine's trick is to appear spontaneous. Flowers are loosely scattered rather than formally arranged, laid on beautiful plates rather than forced into bowls, pinned to a drape of white cotton which is then hung on a wall rather than always being left at table height. 'I like flowers to be mixed together, tumbling and falling,' she says. Treated this way, they become romantic, surreal objects in an artistic landscape. Flowers are also used as drops of colour, like pools of pigment on a canvas. It comes as no surprise that the waxy perfection of an orchid is not something Quartermaine prizes; she prefers the heavy heads of peonies, the crinkled petals of gallicas, or the soft colours and rusted quality of roses that are beginning to turn. She mixes these blooms as she would the papers for one of her collages, layering different colours and shapes. It is an aesthetic that pushes boundaries, liberating the everyday into a fairy-tale dimension.

The words 'arrangement', 'cultivation' and 'formality' have no space in Quartermaine's floral lexicon. Hand-gathered flowers, tied loosely to ribbons, spill down from the ceiling and door handle of a room in a French château. The silk-upholstered salon chairs are painted with Impressionistic sketches of roses. 'There is something about those chairs that makes them look as though they have a personality of their own,' says Quartermaine. 'It is as if they were arriving at a party.'

Quartermaine loves the idea of
flowers 'where you least expect
them'. Placing a real iris over a
flower painted on a plate is typical
of her witty reversals (*left*).
Flowers can be laid on chairs as if
the fabric has sprung to life, or
lightly sketched onto ivory silk as
if they have been pressed into the
pages of a book. And the blooms
need not always be 'perfect' in
the accepted sense. 'There is a
moment when roses are at their
most beautiful, and that is just
when they are beginning to turn.
If it's possible, they are even more
lovely when they are dying.'

For Quartermaine, 'roses are the best perfume. They don't take over a room, they layer it with scent.' They are also living props, adding colour and shape, intensifying a mood, heightening a drama. Piled up on a cake stand they might be a mouthwatering selection from a Viennese pastry shop, the petals made from icing sugar or marzipan (*left*). 'What I really love is the way the whole composition – the stand, the roses – becomes so sculptural.' When pinned to a knot of fabric that has been tied around a chair, a single bloom becomes the chair's sweet-smelling 'corsage' (*right*).

'Flowers have to transport you. They have to take you to places of intrigue and romance.' With her artist's eye, Quartermaine disregards formalities and creates surprising new takes on what flowers can bring to a room. And when she looks at them like this, amazing things start to happen. By placing cut flower-heads on a starched white tablecloth, she neatly translates the floral conventions of traditional English country-house style to something more contemporary. This is chintz for the modern era, the floral shapes literally blossoming out of two dimensions into three.

sources

For further information on any work
featured in this book please contact:

Carolyn Quartermaine
London Design Studio

Tel/Fax 00 44 (0)20 7373 4492

Or write to
PO BOX 12870
London SW5 9WG

For information on Carolyn Quartermaine
textile collection agents and suppliers:

UK, France, Germany, Austria
Charles Koenig Associates
Hornbeam
Dorney Wood Road
Burnham
Bucks SL1 8EH

Tel 00 44 (0)1628 662700
Fax 00 44 (0)1628 667728

Italy
Claudia Norma Longoni

Tel (Mobile) 00 39 (0)3494 654935
Tel 00 39 031 696743

Spain and Portugal
Mengo and Fortes
LG;ENG, Antonio de Almeida
70-7 Sala 406
Porto 4100 065
Portugal

Tel 00 351 22 600 7050
Fax 00 351 22 600 7051

Scandinavia
Interior Plus
Grevturegatan 57
S-11438
Stockholm
Sweden

Tel 00 46 8 665 3118
Fax 00 46 8 665 3119

USA
Christopher Hyland Inc
D&D Building Suite 1710
979 Third Avenue
NY 10022

Tel 001 212 688 6121
Fax 001 212 688 6176

acknowledgments

This title is an abridgement of *Carolyn Quartermaine Unwrapped*. The author would like to thank everyone who worked on the original book, especially Christopher Griffin, Bruce Poole and Olivier Couillaud of Chez Bruce, Caroline Lebeau, Jean Louis Mennesson of Chateau d'Outrelaisse, Zanna (The Ragged School), Annabel Lewis at V.V. Rouleux, Sahco Hesslein, Bodil Tamnhed (who allowed me to keep her funiture for ages), Carolyn Daly, Ruth Forman, Petra Kormann, Claude and François Xavier Lalanne for their magical garden, Anna Thomas, Wild at Heart and Gilding the Lily (flowers), Thrifty Van Rental, Paul Franzosi at Set Pieces, Malabar, Sharyn Storrier-Lyneham, Fix-a-Frame, Pete Smith, John Wright, Nigel Stone, Charles Rutherfoord, Lelievre, Isabelle Corbani, Julie Contreras, Margaret Bradham, Bob Warrens and Bob and Maryse Boxer.

Special thanks go to Jacques Dirand, without whose wonderful eye and expertise this book would not have been the same. Finally, I wish to thank Kate Constable who worked so tirelessly with me on the text.